"Buffam begins with a world that ends, a world that is always ending. This is not despair, but a shrewd mind behind an honest eye that in wry observation creates out of small poems a book of knowledge, 'Little Commentaries,' which show there is no wisdom unsharpened by wounding wit. That motion is an essential motion, and these are essential poems."

—Dan Beachy-Quick

"These poems try to achieve something almost impossible: not to betray the ironic today while celebrating the interiority of a serious meditation. And they succeed in doing it. What a treat!"

—Adam Zagajewski

"Buffam's often deadpan tone is like a magical dustpan that sweeps up the strangest observations and ideas, all worlds to themselves. Her 'Little Commentaries'—'On Piñatas,' 'On Fountains,' and 'On Vanishing Acts' (to name only a few)—are absolute gems, kin to Anne Carson's town poems and Yoko Ono's *Grapefruit*. Buffam's poems tug at new corners of the brain. They're marvelous."

—Matthea Harvey

THE IRRATIONALIST

SUZANNE BUFFAM

CANARIUM BOOKS
ANN ARBOR, BERKELEY, IOWA CITY

SPONSORED BY
THE UNIVERSITY OF MICHIGAN
CREATIVE WRITING PROGRAM

THE IRRATIONALIST

Canarium Books
Ann Arbor, Berkeley, Iowa City
www.canariumbooks.org

The editors gratefully acknowledge the
University of Michigan Creative Writing Program
for editorial assistance and generous support.

Cover: Joshua Edwards, *Gestalt Series (Portrait I)*

Design: Gou Dao Niao

First edition

Printed in the United States of America

ISBN-13: 978-0-9822376-3-2

for Mira

There is another world, but it is inside this one.

Paul Éluard

CONTENTS

I

II

III

I

RUINED INTERIOR

In the beginning was the world.
Then the new world.
Then the new world order

Which resembles the old one,
Doesn't it? Its crumbling
Aqueducts. Its trinkets and shingles.

Its pathways lacquered in fog.
If all we've done is blink a bit
And touch things,

Notice how dust describes
A tin can by not falling
Where it sits, or how a red sleeve

Glimpsed through curtains
Mimics the tip of a flickering
Wing, was the whole day a waste

Or can worth be conferred
On a less than epic urge? Bow-wow
Says the doggie on page two.

Ahoy says the sailor.
Arise says the tired queen
And face the highway,

The donut shops, and the boardwalk.
It rained today. You can see
Perfect inversions of streetlights

Suspended in drops on the window.
You can see the skyline
Trying to hold up the sky.

Don't tell me there's another,
Better place. Don't tell me
There's a sea

Above our dreaming sea
And through the windows of heaven
The rains come down.

IF YOU SEE IT WHAT IS IT YOU SEE

I didn't look at the fire.
I looked into it.

I saw a wall of books
Crash down and bury me

Centuries deep in red leather.
I saw a statue in a park

Shake dust from its fist
And a ship called *Everything*

Sink down on rusted wings.
Ten thousand triangles collapsed

Into a point
And the point was this.

I cannot tell you what I saw.
My catastrophe was sweet

And nothing like yours
Although we may sip

From the same
Broken cup all afternoon.

AMOR FATI

Any idiot can become a genius if she wants it badly enough.

One must study how the crow flies.

One must say to oneself as the crow flies so fly I.

In the dream I am an empty tree. One by one my branches fill
with silent crows that have traveled great distances to
reach me.

Each crow contains a golden seed of knowledge locked in
its craw and by containing them all in my lofty crown
I contain all knowledge of the kingdom.

My attempts to remember are proof in themselves.

At times one must accompany a shadow like the moon above a
field of bitter greens.

In this wretched spirit the pilgrim applies herself and is
rewarded.

"I only felt in the midst of my suffering the presence of a love,"
she explains, "like that which one can read in the smile on a
beloved face."

I can't help what I want.

There is no such thing as a dream that comes true.

Every dream is already true the moment it is dreamed.

THE NEW EXPERIENCE

I was ready for a new experience.
All the old ones had burned out.

They lay in little ashy heaps along the roadside
And blew in drifts across the fairgrounds and fields.

From a distance some appeared to be smoldering
But when I approached with my hat in my hands

They let out small puffs of smoke and expired.
Through the windows of houses I saw lives lit up

With the otherworldly glow of TV
And these were smoking a little bit too.

I flew to Rome. I flew to Greece.
I sat on a rock in the shade of the Acropolis

And conjured dusky columns in the clouds.
I watched waves lap the crumbling coast.

I heard wind strip the woods.
I saw the last living snow leopard

Pacing in the dirt. Experience taught me
That nothing worth doing is worth doing

For the sake of experience alone.
I bit into an apple that tasted sweetly of time.

The sun came out. It was the old sun
With only a few billion years left to shine.

HAPPY HOUR

I'll have an Icecap.
Make it a double.

Bring me a Fog on the River,
A Niagara Falls on the rocks,

And a Tempest with a chaser of Hail.
I don't want to be rescued.

I want to crawl through a honeycomb
Of subglacial passageways,

Shove my head under God's faucet
And keep chugging until I pass out.

I want thirst to drink me.
I want to come back as a bucket of blood.

OCCASIONAL POEM

Today is the thirteen thousand, one hundred and forty-first day of the rest of my life.

There is no way to know how many beans are in the jar without removing them one by one.

If I find it harder to learn the future tense than the younger students in my Spanish class do, it is because so much more of my life resides in the past.

Still I try to live in the moment, where everything is endlessly happening at once.

The earth spins, the curtain lifts, clouds appear to be floating, and yet they are, in fact, constantly falling.

To be ahead of one's time may be the same as being very far behind it.

When he saw the bison leaping off the walls at Lascaux, Picasso turned to his guide and lamented the achievements of modern art.

"We have discovered nothing," he is reported to have said.

And yet today is different from yesterday.

Yesterday only contained itself and the days leading up to it, while today contains itself, yesterday, plus all the endless days before that.

Let us celebrate.

Let us separate the movement from the moving thing.

DEATH TOLL RISES IN BLACK SEA SINKING

From where I stand
The world is a warm blue bath.

I can wash my feet in it.
I can pick a cloud

Any cloud
And watch it nudge a mast

Across a harbor of light.
I have the potential

For offspring inside me
And if it is desire that I lack

I can sit down on a rock
And wait for my lack

To dissolve.
I can do so

And so I do so
Waiting with my feet

At the edge of the bath
Until at length it is time

To lug my body home.
There I read about a storm

In the east
In a story from the west

About a boatload of sailors
Who sank that the water would rise.

THE SOLITARY ANGLER

One day I woke up
And did not fear the old gods.

I called the number on my fridge
And when the movers arrived

I gave them everything.
On my way out of town

I spat into the wind
And did not linger to see where it landed.

Who can say for sure
If the dream has ended or begun?

A frail dimness rims my craft.
Stars swim to the surface of a bottomless well

And sink when I take my eyes off them.
There is no greater calamity

Than to underestimate the strength of your enemy.
The ancients saw the stars

And called them angels.
They turned everything else into a clock.

I say wear a watch if you must
But don't count on it.

THE ARENA

The judges invite me to enter a contest of wits.

If I win, I will be ashamed of myself for having stooped to enter such an unworthy contest in the first place.

If I lose, I will be ashamed of my not being the one to throw down her laurels in disgust.

The only solution seems to be to avoid the arena entirely.

And yet, not to venture at all seems a concession to anticipatory shame—a shameful position in its own right.

To compete or not to compete: this question has dogged mankind since the first hollow scepter was whittled from a bone.

I will have to turn my shame into a point of pride, I see.

I go home and take off my pants, hang a fun-house mirror from my bathroom door, and force myself to eat soup with a spork.

I call myself every bad word I know.

I heap scorn upon myself by the shovelful until I grow so heavy with shame I can barely lift my body into bed.

By the end of the week I feel ready to submit.

But when I show up to take my place at the podium, I discover the contest has ended.

There is cheering in the stands. I am sentenced to reign in a kingdom of sand.

PLACEBO

It is possible to die of fright after being bitten by a non-venomous snake.

Also, in some cultures, to kill a man by pointing a bone at his heart.

These are two severe examples of the nocebo effect—from the Latin for "I will harm." A third is when I forget to wear my lucky orange scarf and lose at craps.

William James writes that often enough our faith beforehand in an uncertified result *is the only thing that makes the result come true.*

How often is often enough?

Will faith alone finish this poem?

When he ran out of morphine on the Tunisian front, Henry Beecher injected dying soldiers with saline instead. At the time he was relying on the strength of faith alone, but what he could not have known back in 1943 was that this solution in fact released a pain-relieving substance in the patient's aching brain.

When asked to discuss his religious beliefs, Luis Buñel replied: I'm an atheist, thank God.

Despair comes from failing to believe new things are possible.

Science: one bold leap after another, suspended by a theory of invisible strings.

Obecalp: what the doctor scrawls on the prescription pad when the pharmacy runs out of science.

Plato believed that to release another person from ignorance despite their initial reluctance was a great and noble thing—and yet every day he woke up and lived in the world as if it were real.

Asleep beneath the sirens and the clashing of arms, who hears the angels gently plucking their inaudible tune?

Who sees the black dog running through the night?

TO LIVE HERE

Paul Éluard

I built a fire, the blue sky having abandoned me.
A fire to befriend.
A fire to introduce me to the winter night.
A fire to live better.

I fed it what the day had fed to me.
Forests, foliage, wheat fields, vines.
Nests and their birds, houses and their keys.
Insects, flowers, furs, festivals.

I lived with the solitary sound of crackling flames.
With the solitary perfume of their heat.
I was like a boat coursing in closed water.
Like the dead I had but one element.

INFINITIVE INTERIOR

To be small among voices.
To wear the black hat.
To kneel in the shavings.
To speak of the nameless blue flowers.
To eat them.
To retreat to the torn red interior.
To hear the low engines approaching.
To button.
To hammer.
To have.
To have not.
To have sat by the sea and been rewarded with a pair of
    glinting wings.
To have held out for more.
To have had it.
To have held out for less.

IDEAL WORLD

Nothing matters in an ideal world.
Not the stones you skip,
Not the fat birds overhead.

Run your fingers through the sand all day.
Lie still as a ship at the bottom of the sea.
Stick out your tongue

And taste the wrecked century
In a melting snowcone purchased for a peso.
All you taste is the taste of it.

Light plucks the coins from your eyes,
The heart spends its store
On a few everlastings

Jutting from cracks in the boardwalk.
Call it a kingdom nevertheless.
Watch the light black canopy

Lower from the west
Where a rust-stained tanker spins
A slow pirouette en route to oblivion

Via Sudan.
If you feel lonely
It's because you were borne this way.

If there are clouds here
They must be ideal clouds.
Clouds you can see through.

II

LITTLE COMMENTARIES

There is no one center of the universe.
Nicolaus Copernicus, *Commentariolus*

ON POSSIBILITY

Here comes the train from Tehuantepec
Bringing lovers and rice.
Bringing last night's dream of floating ponies
To today's rusty gate.

See the faces at the station look up.
See the mystery deepen.
There is no train from Tehuantepec.
Here it comes!

ON NECESSITY

As a young man Galileo
Understood very well
The workings of the pendulum

But not until he was an old man
Approaching
The hour

Of his death
Did he devise
The pendulum clock.

ON SHORTCUTS

I know a painter
Who fills every canvas with sky.
This makes his landscapes look lonely
And his figures bereft.
It's a shortcut, he concedes.
Like adding wings to men
Or putting birds in poems.

ON ATTACHMENT

A house burns all night
In the middle of a field.
A beautiful sight
Even if the burning house
Does happen to be mine.
Sooner or later
All burning houses will be mine.

ON THE FIRE SERMON

Burning burning burning burning
Quotes T. S. Eliot
A man so famed
For his chilly demeanor
Not even his pipe
Seemed to give off smoke.

ON VALLEYS

To be a valley
Find a hill
And lie down at its feet.

ON CLOUDS

To be a cloud
Find a hill
And swallow it.

ON THE ENLIGHTENMENT

Take the thing you love most and cut it up.
Arrange the parts carefully
According to the picture in your head.
Now shine your mind at them.
If their laws come striding boldly forth at you
You will soon become a great man of your time.
If instead they lie there on the table bleeding beauty
You are probably a poet or a child.

ON MOONLIGHT

Moonlight fills the bathroom sink.
If a person could drink from it
She would be her own ghost.

ON GHOSTS V. ZOMBIES

Soul without a body or body without a soul?
Like choosing between an empty lake
And the same empty lake.

ON ABSTRACT EXPRESSIONISM

Ad Reinhardt
Filled his black canvases
With everything he knew
About Modern Art.

Robert Rauschenberg
Emptied his white canvases
Of everything he knew
About Modern Art.

Together they express
Everything and Nothing
There is to know about art.

ON NEGATIVE CAPABILITY

A man and a woman
Side by side

Not speaking
Not not speaking

Cross a moonlit plaza
Without plans.

ON LOVE POEMS

A friend says relationships
Are only good for two poems:
One at the beginning
And one at the end.

Stevens says better to peddle
Pineapples than write love poems
Unless you happen to be
In love, that is.

When your lover shows up
With a basket of fruit
Thank him in advance
For the poem you will one day receive.

ON FIRST LINES

The first line should pry up
A little corner of the soul

As the first ray of daylight
Pries open the sleeper's lids.

ON QUANDARINESS

I do not know which to prefer
The beauty of Nova Scotia
Or the beauty of France.
Ducks landing on the saltmarsh
Or poached in their fat on my plate.

ON DINING IN PARIS

Take small bites.
Chew your food before swallowing.
Do not expect the waiter to congratulate you.

ON DRINKING IN PARIS

Greet the new Beaujolais
With a mixture of fondness and disdain
Like a childhood friend from the provinces
Or yet another Oscar-winning picture
Starring Gérard Depardieu.

ON PARAKEETS

Practice concentrating on an empty stomach.
Practice making love with a terrible sunburn.
Practice walking with little dried peas in your shoes.
Sprinkle sand in your food.
Sprinkle salt in your tea.
Pitch your tent in a howling gale.
Soon you will be ready to live in the house on the hill
Next door to the house full of parakeets.

ON COULD

There is no cake in the oven, alas
But a small bit of effort
Could put one there.

ON TRAVEL

Not past my Father's Gate
She Vowed—
As she Closed her Eyes
And lit out for Zanzibar.

ON BORGES

Put one dream
Inside another.

ON OBLIVION

The most harrowing thing
About outer space

Claim the astronauts
Who have set foot there

Is not so much the darkness
As the silence.

Beethoven heard it
And composed his final symphony.

On opening night
He kept his back to the audience

And when the orchestra reached
The music's echoing close

He continued to conduct for several bars.
Embarrassment

Rippled through the room
Like cosmic wind.

But not through Beethoven
By then light years away.

ON ROMANTICISM

Out of nowhere
Blows a baleful wind
To explain your heart to you.

ON FLAGS

Few things are more stirring
Than a flag in the wind.
A problem of aesthetics vs. ethics.
All morning I study
A tea towel drying on the line.
A flag without a country
Is like desire without an end.

ON METAPHOR

When Job laments that *the Lord*
Hath put my brethren far from me
It is up to you to decide
If he is speaking metaphorically.

ON INVECTIVE

Fuck you and the horse you rode in on
Is often just another way of saying come back.

ON AD CAMPAIGNS IN THE UNDERWORLD

Bet you can't eat just one
Smiled Pluto
As he held out his handful of pain.

ON IMPOSSIBILITY

I try to write "automatically"
But keep stopping to look at the sky.
Words are in it
And a great blue silence
That fills the distance between.

ON NOVA SCOTIA

Dusk spread its glaucous wing over the salt marsh.
Here is a good place to stop, said the King.
The ignorant hills look familiar.
And the darkness shall be made new.

ON SEVILLE

Every tree is an orange tree.
Every pigeon a dove.

ON GEOLOGICAL TIME

Enjoy the view while you can,
Mt. Everest.

ON MIDDLE NAMES

Victor
Selwyn
Hamish
Adeline
Aurora
Somerset
Loomis
And Stearns
Set out for a picnic
Beneath the green
Never trees.

ON NORMANDY

Fate piles up
On the bloody Norman shore.
If you must swim there
Swim on your back.

ON LAST LINES

The last line should strike like a lover's complaint.
You should never see it coming.
And you should never hear the end of it.

ON VANISHING ACTS

The magician says watch closely.
The lover says close your eyes.

ON DURATION

To cross an ocean
You must love the ocean
Before you love the far shore.

ON PIÑATAS

No point in swinging the bat
Unless the blindfold's secure.

ON FIREWORKS

Radiant pitchforks thunder in the now
Trailing specters of is.

ON AMBITION

Like love
It grows impatient
Of both rivals and delays.

ON GOLD

Unlike love
Its value increases
When it sits in the vault.

ON YESTERDAY

Of all the bright fruits in the market
I bought only one.
Now my peach
Is a pit.
Plant it deeper.

ON WINTER

It is a good rule of thumb
To leave your house at least once.
If you have a little dog
You can take him for a little walk.
If a big dog, a big walk.
But you cannot cross an open field
Where snow is melting
Without growing a little bit
Older with every step.

ON FOUNTAINS

Joy alone upholds the moment
When the sparkling ascent
Is overwhelmed.

ON JOY

Joy unmixed with sorrow
Is like a fountain turned off at night.

ON INVERSE RELATIONS

The pleasure I feel
When I say the word "trousers"
Is equal, exactly
To the discomfort I feel
When I say the word "slacks."

ON MOVING DAY

Two houses stand aloof
In their emptiness.

The same dusty sunlight
Licks the floorboards

Of your future and your past.
It is good

To be homeless
For an hour.

45

ON EXILE

One of the richest men in Rome
Seneca knew many pleasures in life.

In particular, it is said
He loved to dine on quail

At a citrus-wood table
With ivory legs.

But he also knew
The fickle winds of Empire.

Far from home
Without a friend

Or lover near
With but a thin gruel

Before you
And plank for a pillow

Recall his recollection
Of these pleasures in a letter

To his mother from the tower:
Between them and me

I have kept a wide gap.

ON EVOLUTION

Place your face
Into your hands.
A perfect fit!

ON RELATIVITY

A pygmy hippopotamus
Is roughly the size
Of a large family dog.

A capybara
Is an enormous guinea pig
Roughly the size

Of a very small horse.
The smallest horses
Wear very small shoes

Roughly the size
A fairly large person would wear
During infancy

A brief phase
If you are human
A lifetime

If you are a fly.

ON THE NEW DARKNESS

What's wrong
With the Old Darkness?

ON SATISFACTION

Make lists
Of things you have already done.
Pleasure exists
In crossing them off one by one.

ON LA GIOCONDA

Crowds press in to glimpse her terrible smile.
What diet of secrets sustains it?

The crowds soon tire
And retreat to the buzzing café.

Aloof behind her varnish and her bulletproof veil
She casts her gaze on nothing now—

The greatest, said Da Vinci
Among all great things found here among us.

ON IMPEDIMENTS

Children play ball
In the crowded plaza

Not in spite of the crowd
But because of it.

ON RIDING BACKWARDS ON TRAINS

Through the red hills and over green dells
The shock of it shakes from you
Endless farewells.

There goes a fountain. There goes a goat.
Back to the future
Heart in your throat.

ON THE VERB ESPERAR

In Madrid you may wait your whole life for salvation
While hoping all day for your turn at the bank.

ON FORGIVENESS

It is best to forgive all sins in advance
Because afterwards it can be hard.

ON ADVICE

Do not offer advice
And do no solicit it.
Seek wisdom within.
But do be sure to bring
A pair of long underwear
For those long cold hours
In the desert at night.

ON SPACE TRAVEL

Not to see the frozen heavens up close
But to see our leaky planet from afar.

ON COMMON SENSE

Aristarchus of Samos
Sealed his fate as a footnote
By pointing out the movement of the Earth around the Sun
To Aristotle of Stagira
Who pointed out birds in the sky
Keeping pace with it.

ON ST. AUGUSTINE

Love and do what you will
Is a dangerous slogan
To plaster on the walls
Of a freshman dorm in spring.

ON MADAME BOVARY

Misanthropy starts at home.
So great was Flaubert's
Grasp of pitiless fact
He cast himself as a woman
And punished her with all
The love in his heart.

ON BEAUTY

Noon comes hammering down on the harbor
Ringing all its bells.
Masts tip
This way and that
Scratching God's name on the vault.

ON THE SEINE

Beggar sailor soldier thief
And the dregs of Saint Joan
Slip black as God's mirror
Beneath your bright bateaux mouches.

ON SUICIDE

People who commit suicide don't fail to believe in life.
They fail to believe in death.

ON THE LOGIC OF DREAMS

While in dreams it is true
Anything can happen

Dreams often seem bound
By inexplicable rules.

In this way they resemble Poetry
Astronomy, Geometry, Love . . .

ON CHURCH BELLS

Every
Hour
On
The
Hour
What
Stirs
This
Sleepy
Nowhere
Is
Old
News

ON HUMMINGBIRDS

The smaller the heart the swifter the wings.

ON WHITE FLOWERS

By moonlight the lily dominates the field.

ON CLEAR NIGHTS

At most two thousand stars
Can be seen with the naked eye from earth.

A difficult number to grapple with.
Too large, and, on the other hand, too small.

A simple mathematical equation
May throw the problem into relief.

Consider a battlefield.
The fighting has ended

And the bodies lie still in the grass.
How many dead soldiers

Equal the sky overhead?

ON ANTIGONE

Law spoke
And the land bit its lip.
Why spit in the wind?
Love too is a law.

ON WHERE YOU LIVE

Somewhere I have never been
That you

Bent over your books
In snug bronze lamplight

Beyond
Night's silvered reminiscenses

Will never see.

ON IRRATIONAL NUMBERS

Ahoy cries the sunrise
To the sea's flagging captains
Among whom you number
Infinity plus one.

ON PARADISE

No Then.
No My.
No Soul.
No Like.
No To.
No The.
No Lark.
No At.
No Break.
No Of.
No Day.
No Arising.
No From.
No Sullen.
No Earth.
No Sings.
No Hymns.
No At.
No Heavens.
No Gate.

ON EVERYONE

Everyone loves a balloon in the sky.
It is head-shaped and floating away.
It knows not why it goes
Nor where it will be when it gets there.
It wags its little tail and disappears.

III

THE WISE MAN

I am not a wise man. This makes my life difficult in certain
ways. But in other ways it simplifies things. I find it hard to sit
still very long before I get up and wander the halls in my hat for
example. On the other hand I stay warm and keep moving.
Could these ways be the same way? A wise man could tell you.
A wise man would look out his window and see not a row of
low clouds rolling east like a trainload of coal through a
crossroads, but a lit glimpse of the infinite, the wise man's only
home. A wise man might think of his childhood and smile.
Often in a quandary I ask myself what would a wise man do?
A fool sees not the same tree that a wise man sees, said a wise
man, and when I look out at the spruce I wonder what a wise
man sees. A wise man might laugh at such questions. As for me
I laugh often, but I don't get the joke.

THE TRUE BELIEVER

There are only two ways of reacting to life. Every scripture in the world will tell you this. Choose the wrong one and no amount of digging will save you. Before me an old woman plucks a stubborn hair from her cheek. Behind me a child weeps into her spinach. I'm the one on her knees with a shovel, wiping starbursts of spit from her chin. Each day rises with the promise of news. Sometimes it isn't time for so long I forget what I'm hoping it's time for.

TRYING

For a long time we looked at the world and thought not. Then we looked at our lives and thought maybe. Now we are trying. We bought a new set of sheets for the bed. We bought a thermometer and a book.

*

I find the book on the whole reassuring. It gives lots of examples using real-life names like Gail, Audrey, and Dr. Smith, as well as comic touches here and there like Dr. Rhea Sure, who keeps popping up on Gail's chart. But Appendix K does contain some trying phrases. What, for example, is a Hamster Egg Penetration Assay? What is Nonstimulated Oocyte Retrieval In (Office) Fertilization? What is the Male Factor? What is Within Normal Limits?

*

If procreation were a matter to be decided purely on the basis of rational thought, would the human race still exist? Schopenhauer thought not. Every evening, rain or shine, he would walk his poodle, Atma, for two solid hours through the streets of pre-war Frankfurt, trying to imagine a world as sterile and crystalline as the moon.

*

I try to find it reassuring that Gail is thirty-eight.

*

After swallowing a tiny vial of poison that had weakened over time around his neck, Napoleon escaped his island exile on Elba in the autumn of 1812, having built up a tiny island empire there, replete with tiny army and navy, tiny copper mines, and fields of tiny cabbages and beets. When his ship touched shore he rode bravely out to meet his former soldiers alone and dismounted to address them. The entire Grande Armée turned around on the spot and escorted Le Petit Corporal back to Paris, where he renewed his ancient vow to die trying.

*

This morning I tried on my bikini while my husband walked the dog. I turned around and used a compact to study my backside in the mirror above the sink. The mirror, perhaps mercifully, was dusty, and I did not get a good look.

*

The majority of husbands remind me of an orangutan trying to play the violin, said Balzac.

*

My husband, thank heavens, is cooperative. He has even read a few pages of the book. And yet sometimes I worry that it is his fault. That either he is not trying hard enough, or that he is trying too hard, or that no matter how hard he tries or does not try it is his Male Factor that is the problem.

While searching for advice on overcoming adversity, I find a book called *Tom Cruise: Overcoming Adversity*. I learn that the public only sees the glamour—but Phelan Powell shows the significant obstacles Tom Cruise has overcome in order to live his life of pampered opulence. In Cruise's case dyslexia was one obstacle—it nearly cost him the part of the barman in *Cocktail* (he thought it was a film about cockatiels and told his agent he "didn't do parrots") and he bought his own wildebeest to research the part of Lieutenant Maverick Mitchell in *Top Gnu*. This description is a direct cut-and-paste from an Amazon.com review by a reader named Henry Raddick in London, UK, who gives the book five stars and titles his review: "Pig-ignorance no bar to fame and fortune." I try to picture what Henry Raddick looks like, and does he live with his mother.

*

The book lives on the back of the toilet and I try to visit it from time to time throughout the day. Sometimes I just look at it. Sometimes I go in there and sit down and open it at random and get lost looking at the pictures. The follicle develops. The egg begins its journey down the tube . . .

*

The human soul, wrote Aristotle in his treatise on ethics, has an irrational element which is shared with the animals, and a rational element which is distinctly human. In order to live a virtuous life one must try to achieve some sort of balance between them. In his *Poetics*, however, Aristotle points out that it is exclusively the irrational upon which the wonderful depends for its chief effects.

*

Every morning, before getting up to make breakfast, I record my temperature down to the tenth of a degree on a chart, and draw a line between yesterday's and today's. I compare my progress with the sample in the book and try not to worry.

*

People who believe in God will tell you that "trying" to believe will not work. And yet some believers insist that simply wanting to believe is enough. I keep flipping back and forth between trying and wanting to try.

*

In his early twenties it was said that Jean Cocteau could bring himself to orgasm without touching himself, purely by the power of his imagination. Here I am trying to live, he wrote, or rather, I am trying to teach the death within me to live.

*

When my two oldest friends write to tell me their good news, I try not to let my jealousy show, and sprinkle exclamation marks liberally throughout my replies.

*

Often, I have read, the very act of "trying" can undermine one's prospects of success. This makes trying difficult. The trick, they say, is to try without actually "trying." Having finally decided to start trying we must keep on trying while trying not to feel like we are "trying" at all. We must above all try not to worry. Sometimes I worry that I am not trying not to try hard enough.

*

It is one thing to marvel at the miracle of life, but quite another to try to explain it. Almost every freshman biology textbook printed in the last fifty years contains the famous Miller-Urey experiment of 1953, in which Harold Urey and Stanley Miller tried to simulate early atmospheric conditions on Earth, in order to see what they could generate by adding an electrical spark. What they discovered were amino acids, the basic building blocks of life. From there, most books lead straight into a discussion of evolution, prompting the student to conclude that scientists have thus proven life can be created from a few nonliving chemicals. We tell this story to beginning students of biology, admitted Nobel laureate George Wald in his 1954 article, *The Origin of Life*, as though it represents a triumph of reason over mysticism. In fact, he points out, it is very nearly the opposite.

TRANS-NEPTUNIAN OBJECT

The time and place and manner of my death are three facts
that don't exist yet.

Facts exist for whole centuries and then suddenly cease.

Pluto used to be a planet and now it is a chunk of debris,
number 134340.

My grandmother's house stands on the hill above the sea
where she left it.

When I come back to visit I discover a crater in its place.

This room is full of facts.

All day I let the cat out, let it in, then let it back out again.

I mean this metaphorically.

Some facts never exist.

It is winter.

It is summer.

All night the branches tap at the glass.

TELESCOPIC INTERIOR

Solar wind singing in a bottlecap.
Distant drone of stone
Drilled through for more stone

Less prone to collapse.
Add fire. Add feast days and photons
And glue the whole mess

Together in a nerve net
Swinging through the cosmos on a peg.
If you can sleep through this

Send me a lullaby
From your crib of green dreams.
Down here the weather's red

And the century's turning
Every storm back to port.
At the last resort

They're selling sand as souvenirs.
The roses have never looked lonelier,
Less photogenic, but get this—

They're going ahead with the festival.
They're addressing the peacock dilemma.
They're dredging the harbor.

They're shooting pitchforks at the moon.
Through a cracked telescope
I watch the late show unfold

Its milky arabesque across the deep.
How could I sleep? The brightest star
In the sky tonight is a planet

Called Tomorrow.
I used to live there.
I should know.

THE LAST THING

In one version heaven is a tidy German town.

In another it's a shining patch of glory at the center of the earth.

Read the various accounts and you will learn that happiness consists in greater happiness ahead.

Yet every story about the future becomes, in time, a story about the past.

Another story about the past: you live in a town on the surface of the earth.

Things happen in this town.

A dog barks. A bell rings. A cart overturns on the sidewalk and spills a winter's worth of oranges in your path.

Meanwhile astronomers predict a "Big Rip" in the cosmos resulting in a cold, dark, never-ending end.

What kind of happiness is this?

Drink your coffee.

Unplug your phone.

Don't believe the stories about life outside your town.

THE SOLITARY ANGLER (II)

Ma Yuan of the Song Dynasty was famous for painting "just one corner" of his canvases. His solitary angler sits small as a stone above a dark sea dissolving into mist. The point is, there is much we can't see.

Man should be a windowpane through which God's light can shine. In his dark night, St. John saw this.

So long had it been since he'd seen a woman's foot, when he met Joan Baez, Thomas Merton asked her to remove a shoe. Paradise is still ours but we do not know it, he wrote.

Snow falls on birch trees and the branches bend to earth.

If only I had the tiniest grain of wisdom, wrote Lao Tzu, I should walk in the Great Way, and my only fear would be to stray from it.

My little way, wrote Thérèse de Lisieux, stroking death's sleepy head nestled in the damp folds of her sheets.

The brain is a small grey tissue afloat on a wave. Everything we know and can ever know about existence is there.

Man stands in his own shadow and wonders why it is dark.

One way to know is unknowing, yet another way reports,
which must be different than not knowing.

How else would we know not.

ABSTRACT FIRES

(Mixed media. 1972-present)

#1. Candy canes, tinfoil, flamenco guitar.

#2. Fork, butterfly, dog hair, dust.

#3. Trampoline, harpsichord, rust.

#4. Thumbtacks, chewing gum, forklift, car.

#5. Light bulb, lipstick, ceiling fan, string.

#6. Bathtub, shaving cream, flag.

#7. Disco ball, flashlight, dental floss, diamond ring.

#8. Sand, tin cans, oilcloth rag.

#9. Termites, teacup, artist, microscope.

#10. Sequins, hairdryer, liquid smoke.

#11. Work boots, aquarium, encyclopedia, peach.

#12. Cigarette, rope.

#13. Paper bag, rose.

#14. Glass jug, snow.

DIM-LIT INTERIOR

I'm done crying in my beer about love.

My days of riding the shiny brass school bus are behind me as well.

The changes come slowly but suddenly.

One day the sun will burn so brightly it will turn all our seas into vast boiling vats.

Freedom comes from understanding our inability to change things.

So lead me O Destiny whither is ordained by your decree.

Just please don't force me to vacuum the stairs.

The quiet that follows the storm may be the same as the quiet before it.

Let the wind blow.

Let it blow down each tree on the bright boulevard.

The things I would most like to change are the things that make me believe change is possible.

ENOUGH

I am wearing dark glasses inside the house
To match my dark mood.

I have left all the sugar out of the pie.
My rage is a kind of domestic rage.

I learned it from my mother
Who learned it from her mother before her

And so on.
Surely the Greeks had a word for this.

Now surely the Germans do.
The more words a person knows

To describe her private sufferings
The more distantly she can perceive them.

I repeat the names of all the cities I've known
And watch an ant drag its crooked shadow home.

What does it mean to love the life we've been given?
To act well the part that's been cast for us?

Wind. Light. Fire. Time.
A train whistles through the far hills.

One day I plan to be riding it.

VANISHING INTERIOR

Little patches of grass disappear
In the jaws of lusty squirrels

Who slip into the spruce.
Cars collapse into parts.

Spring dissolves into summer,
The kitten into the cat.

A tray of drinks departs from the buffet
And voilà! the party's over.

All that's left are some pickles
And a sprig of wilting parsley on the rug.

When I think of all those
Gong-tormented Mesozoic seas

I feel a ripple of extinction
And blow a smoke ring through the trees.

Soon there will be nothing left here but sky.
When I think about the fact

I am not thinking about you
It is a new way of thinking about you.

PLAIN GREEK

Fate's wind can be cold it is true.
What is the wind to you
But an impression of wind

A *phantasia*
As Epictetus puts it
In his *Handbook*

A fact you must weather
Like any other fact
Such as daylight adultery taxes

And naturally death.
Face the facts.
They do not matter.

What matters is the use
You put them to.
The *Iliad* consists of nothing but facts.

Epictetus wipes his nose
And explains this
To the students growing restless at his feet.

Fact prompted Paris.
Fact prompted Helen to follow.
If fact had prompted Menelaus

To count his blessings
In the face of Helen's absence
Not only the *Iliad*

Would have been lost to us
But the *Odyssey* too.
When the wind blows

Do not long for warmer climes.
Epictetus puts it
In plain Greek.

Wipe your nose
And do not accuse God.
If all is fire

You may warm your hands
By thrusting them here
Into this burning book.

IDEAL TREE

God is in the forest counting trees.
You are in the city writing poems.
You put a tree in a poem.
A tree without roots or branches
Or squirrels or sap
Without even a shadow
In its crown, for it grows
Without even a crown.
You are so pleased with your poem
And with the sound it makes
When you read it out loud
And when you whisper it
Into your pillow at night
You call your poem
"The Tree of Everlasting Love"
And plant it lovingly
Between the waiting pages
Of an unwritten book.
There it dwells for many years
Untainted by moss or regard.
And when you finally publish
Your book of sad poems
No one even notices the tree.
No one sees it burning coldly
Through all the foggy mornings
Of your misinterpretable world.

A PERFECT EMERGENCY

It was already aflame when I spotted it there in the parking lot.

Kids were standing around throwing sticks at it, kicking dirt in
its face.

All I could do was look on in pity as it thrashed at the air like a
tiny, vengeful sun.

But like a tiny, vengeful sun, the burning bush didn't want
pity. When I approached with my hands in my pockets,
it shook out its golden locks and sang in a language I could
see.

I am the Unburnt Bush! it cried. *I am Burning but Flourishing!
I am Swallowed but I am not Consumed!*

In my head was a page from a musty old book with its useless
list of Latin verbs. Before me I could see all the lives I
might have lived, lined up and leaping through the same
burning gate.

It was a perfect emergency. The only thing worth saving was
the blaze.

ROMANTIC INTERIOR

Wind rips splendor from the trees
And lays it at our feet.
Some of us hungry,

Some of us lucky to be upright at all.
Season past sweetness.
Stuck in the throat with a fork.

A speck in the spectrum
Spins into a wet little planet
Studded with heartlust,

Flooded with pamphlets
For classes on how to forget.
Where Keats sees a reaper

Asleep on the granary floor,
Her scythe set by quietly,
Wind playing games

With the husk of her hair,
I see a dead squirrel.
It's the end of October

And I don't have a costume.
Past lives clutter my closet
A long way from home.

There's a hole in the ground
Where my house used to be.
A hole in my head

Where my heart used to be.
I'm climbing a hillside.
A green patch of laughter.

EXIT

Low cirrocumulus clouds in the west.
War in the east.

Lift teabag from cup.
Add milk.

Ask if it is happiness
Or pleasure you prefer.

Watch the storm churn to the surface.
Shadows gather in the valley below.

To count them is to know their many shapes
Cannot be counted.

They must be numbered among.

ACKNOWLEDGMENTS

Grateful acknowledgment is made to the editors of the following journals who kindly published poems from this manuscript: *Alaska Quarterly Review*, *A Public Space*, *Boston Review*, *Commonline*, *Columbia Poetry Review*, *Court Green*, *Crazyhorse*, *Denver Quarterly*, *Fou*, *jubilat*, *MiPoesias*, *Pleiades*, *Ryga*, *SmallStations*, and *Washington Square*.

Additionally, some of this work was represented in anthologies, and I am grateful to the editors of these as well: *Canarium 1* (Canarium Books) and *VERSschumggel / reVERSible* (Wonderhorn / Editions du Noroît / Literaturwekstatt).

Several poems in this manuscript were published in a chapbook, *Interiors*, with art by Shawn Kuruneru (Montreal: Delirium Press, 2006).

"Dim-Lit Interior" was featured in the Poem of the Week section in February 2008 on the website of the Parliamentary Poet Laureate.

Thanks to my family, friends, teachers, and colleagues for their love and guidance throughout the writing of this book. In particular, thank you to Robyn Schiff, for her sharp editorial insights, and to Josh Edwards, for his vision and labor.

Thank you, Chicu. Ideal reader.

Suzanne Buffam was born and raised in Canada. Her previous collection of poetry, *Past Imperfect*, was published in 2005 by House of Anansi Press, and won the Gerald Lampert Memorial Award for the best first book of poetry published in Canada that year. She lives in Chicago, and teaches at the University of Chicago.